Drum
Majors
for
Justice

BLACK HISTORY 101

MOBILE MUSEUM

101 Quotes by African American
Politicians

Library of Congress Cataloging-in-Publication Data
Drum Majors For Justice/Khalid el Hakim
ISBN-9780984666881

Compiled by Khalid el-Hakim
founder of the Black History 101 Mobile Museum

Cover design: Lindsey Naylor
Publishing Consultant: Intelligent Consulting

Table of Contents

▴▴▴

ACKNOWLEDGMENTS

Thank you:

Family: My wonderful wife Tasleem el-Hakim, Mom, Clifton, Larry, David, Elena, Keisha, BreAna, Monique, Maryum, Khalilah and the whole Millben family, Bell Family, and Turner family.

My road warriors: Carl Stubbs, Freeling Guinn, Craig Huckaby, Umar bin Hassan, The Last Poets, Professor Griff (the truest soldier for the people I know!), Omari King Wise, Vivee Francis, Duminie Deporres, Keeli Lackey, Erik Perry, Geoff Devereaux, O.A. Hyatt and 3rd Stone from the Sun, PROOF, 5 Ela, 3rd Eye Open family, Supa Emcee, Versiz, 1st Born, jessica Care moore, Kyle Burch, Sam Greenlee, Amer Ahmed, Derrick Jenkins and Mr. Gregory Reed. Having you all in my corner over the years has been a blessing beyond words.

Mentors: Dr. Jesse Eugene Huff, Raymond Gant, Minister Malik Shabazz, Dawud Muhammad, Dr. David Pilgrim, Angela Kenyatta, Dr. James Cornett, Tyree Guyton, and Paul Lee. It is because of your inspiration, insight, words of encouragement and example that I've been able to fulfill my dreams.

Finally this is a very SPECIAL THANKS to the many people who have made donations of artifacts, financial, and in-kind support to the Black History 101 Mobile Museum over the years. I can't thank you enough for seeing the vision and blessing me with your precious gifts. Willie Williams, Danielle-Martinique, Amié Césaire, Christine Otten (Amsterdam), Marco Bakker(Amsterdam), Orisanmi Burton, Daisy Elliot, Prince Whipper Whip, Fez of Added Flava(Australia), HipHopDX.com, Lori Robinson, Njia Kai, Darren Nichols, Jenenne Whitfield and The Heidelberg Project, Bro. Raheem, Dan Hoops, Invincible, Freeway, Kevin "Natural" Westbrook, Janet Burch, Awesome Dre, BOSS, Derrick May, Alan Sterling, Chuck D, KRS-ONE, OneBeLo, Dr. Robert Shumake, Marvin X, Barbara Rose Collins, David Hilliard, Cheryl White and my Detroit Lions Academy family, Kahn Davison, Mr. and Mrs. Lackey, Chazz

Miller, John and Alicia (The Artist Village Family), Mr. Don and
Hilda Vest, Sharif Liwaru, Aku Kadogo, Dr. Sharon Helm, QDIII,
Mike Wird, DJ Los, Gabe Gonzales, Ill Uno, Kwasi, Erik Perry,
ESHAM, J Hill, Miles Dixon, Andrei Nichols, Michael Griffin, Joe
Taglioli, Rudy and Carlito Hill, Daisy Elliott, Ice T and Coco,
James Muhammad, James Young, Nefertiti and Jelani (Truth
Bookstore), Lisbet Tellefsen, Erika Huggins, Simona Vasquez,
Champtown, Rich Stringer, Kalimah Johnson, Lottie Spady, DJ
SloPoke, Traci Currie, Dawn Demps, Bro. Kwantu, Melinda Jones,
Nate Spencer, Bill Adler, Peggy Woods, James Wheeler, Chaka
Rae, Emani and Husayn Bey, Shawn P, Tim Caldwell, Atarah
Freedom, Jennie Kay, Doug Coombe, Swandolyn Carroll-Howard,
Brother Robert Saleem, Bertha McNeil, Sherrie Fuller Sis. Wanita
Shakoor, Frederick Gooding, Jr., Mike Ellison, Fred Safford, Ernie
Paniccioli, Linda Burton, Rhonda Sewell, Wilma Dunlap, and Dr.
Barbara Emerson Williams.

FOREWORD

I've recently become more fascinated with deconstructing the black voice. Who has the right to claim it/bottle it/copy it...even quote it? For the past 20 years Khalid El-Hakim has been collecting the black voice with his passionate work building the Black History 101 Mobile Museum. His educational, revolutionary museum, which literally boasts several thousand pieces of black history memorabilia, has toured all over the country and abroad for over a decade.

What we say and how we say it, becomes an embedded definition and history for a particular group or culture forever. In **Drum Majors For Justice**, collector and author, Khalid El-Hakim offers a brilliant collection of 101 quotes by politicians on the front lines of change in this country.

There is a need for the deep excavation of double consciousness that inevitably comes from being black and political in America. From a frontline activism perspective, it is sometimes simply about discovering the reason why Malcolm smiled with great intention, as he fired words as weapons from his mouth. His speeches were a series of back to back t-shirt ready quotes. Malcolm would win over audiences with his compelling oratory skills, just as current President Barack Obama won the world over with his great ability to take over a global room.

Still, there isn't a voice more complex than the one of a black politician in the United States of America. From grassroots activism to Washington DC, there is a fascination with holding office and the power it holds to be a place of great pride and sometimes of horrid shame in the Black community.

Like the revered short-form poem, Haiku, the "quote" is something magical and powerful and can stand the test of time if passed down through oral history, gossip, film, and if we are lucky enough, inside the pages of a book, so our future children can one day hold it in their hands.

In this historical poignant collection, we hear from the first African American Mayor of Detroit, Michigan, Coleman A. Young, Thurgood Marshall, Maxine Waters, and Barbara Jordan, the first African American woman from the south to be elected to the U.S. House of Representatives.

I'm not a big fan of politicians, but there are those certain "Drum Majors' who force us to recognize their important work while they are/were in office. This is after all, a prestigious place we had to fight for in current American history. This definitive collection highlights the words and political force

behind warrior women like Maxine Waters.
Waters has been a constant inspiration for
many politically minded young brown
women in this country. Still, one of my
favorite quotes is from my comrade, Cynthia
McKinney, who said:

"Ever since I came to Congress in 1992,
there are those who have been trying to silence
my voice. I've been told to "sit down and shut
up" over and over again. Well, I won't sit
down and I won't shut up until the full and
unvarnished truth is placed before the
American people."

McKinney, who ran for President with long
time grassroots activist, Rosa Clemente in
2008, is an example and great teaching
reference of the power and fear of the black
feminine voice in American politics.

Quotes represent a phenomenal moment in history and when delivered correctly, they become timeless, embedded markers of our existence. Drum Majors for Justice compiles 101 of some of these moments to help us reflect, and most importantly, insure that we never forget the struggle and sacrifice it takes to make real change in this country and the world.

It makes sense that Khalid, an important young educator and father from the City of Detroit, who carries a deep sense of self love, a great respect for Hip Hop, and an understanding of the importance of us preserving our own culture, would create an inspirational collection of quotes that will serve our youth population so wonderfully.

Welcome to Black History 101.

-*Jessica Care Moore*
CEO, Publisher and Author
Moore Black Press Inc.
www.mooreblackpress.com

INTRODUCTION

On October 16, 1995, while standing in the midst of more than one million Black men on the National Mall in Washington, DC, I became more politically aware in a way I never imagined. For the first time, Black men in America didn't ask "the powers that be" for permission to take a day to come together and declare as a group to take responsibility, atone to their communities and deal with their mutual challenges.

The historic Million Man March was the
event that sealed my commitment to
publicly share a small private collection
of Black memorabilia that I had been
passionate about collecting since 1991.
For the first time in American history,
Black men heeded a call to come to the
Nation's capital to exercise their
Constitutional right to peacefully
assemble; and those same men made a
pledge to work for self-improvement and
to recommit to their communities. Many
critics predicted that the Million Man
March would not bring about lasting
change. I would challenge any one of
those critics to observe the profound
change that I personally experienced—a
transformation that ultimately led to
this odyssey.

At the Million Man March, the idea of a
Black History 101 Mobile Museum was
crystallized. Prior to that life-changing

event, I was a private collector of Black
memorabilia and just shared artifacts that
I collected among friends and family.
Those friends and family members can tell
stories of me "holding them hostage" on
road trips by taking detours to antique
shops and other out-of-the-way venues to
search literally for hours on end for the
next relevant artifact that would help to
tell the story of the Black experience in
America; a story that has largely been
omitted from United States history.

The majority of my political awareness
prior to the Million Man March was
derived from the messages infused in Hip
Hop music. I was heavily influenced by
The Last Poets, KRS-One, Rakim, Public
Enemy, Ice Cube and X-Clan. One of the
most powerful examples of Hip-Hop's
impact on a major policy change was
Public Enemy's "By the Time I Get to

Arizona". That song almost single handedly forced the state of Arizona to authorize a statewide holiday to pay respect to the national holiday celebrating the legacy of Martin Luther King, Jr. Arizona was one of the last states to institute a holiday honoring Dr. King; and the holiday finally came about through a popular voter affirmation fully nine years after the national holiday was signed into law. The social pressure that the state of Arizona received from the Hip Hop generation also showed that Hip Hop had the power to make a difference.

The story of Black politicians throughout American history is one that has truly tested the meaning of the words and ideas laid out in the United States Constitution and defined by the first words of the Preamble: "We the People". Many Americans today do not know that it was U. S. Congressman John Conyers, a Democrat from Detroit, Michigan, who was the first to introduce the resolution to make the King Day holiday. Mr. Convers

presented the resolution on the floor of the
House of Representatives just four days after
Martin Luther King was assassinated on
April 4, 1968. It was through the American
political process that fifteen years later the
holiday was written into law.

One of my biggest challenges as a Social
Studies teacher in the Detroit Public Schools
for thirteen years was introducing the
principles and foundations of American
government to my students on the eastside of
Detroit. In the social studies curriculum, the
core democratic values are central to students
thoroughly understanding the American
political system. In teaching core democratic
values, I always used examples of African
American politicians who exemplified these
core democratic values. Being able to speak
truth to power in America when it was
possible to lose everything, even your life for
doing so, has always been inspiring to me. It
is critically important for our youth to learn

the stories of those who came before us and who left a blueprint for success.

The purpose of this book is to inspire all people, but especially students, to become aware of the legacies others have left behind and to become inspired to Personally engage in the political process. It is my hope that the quotes contained in this book resonate with the readers as much as they have done with me. It is only through this engagement that we can all become the "drum majors for justice" that Rev. Dr. Martin Luther King, Jr. envisioned.

Khalid el-Hakim, Founder
Black History 101 Mobile Museum
www.blackhistory101mobilemuseum.com

ABOUT KHALID EL-HAKIM

Khalid el-Hakim is an educator, activist, and founder of the Black History 101 Mobile Museum. The Black History 101 Mobile Museum is a collection of over 5,000 original artifacts that spans the Black experience from slavery to Hip Hop. The Black History 101 Mobile Museum travels to colleges /universities, K-12 schools, libraries, conferences, and cultural events across the country.

**All of the photos presented in this book are of original artifacts from the archives of the Black History 101 Mobile Museum.

COLEMAN A. YOUNG

*1ST African American Mayor of
Detroit, Michigan*

~ 3 ~

I've learned over a period of years
there are setbacks when you come up
against the immovable object;
sometimes the object doesn't move.

~C. Young

There is no brilliant single stroke that is going to transform the water into wine or straw into gold.

~C. Young

You can't look forward and backward at the same time.

~C. Young

We need to dream big dreams,
propose grandiose means if we are to
recapture the excitement, the
vibrancy, and pride we once had.

~C. Young

BLACK HISTORY 101
MOBILE MUSEUM

Courage is one-step ahead of fear.

~C. Young

CARL STOKES

City of Cleveland

CARL B. STOKES
MAYOR

October 18, 1968

Dear Sandy:

I am delighted to be able to send you the autographed picture you requested in your letter, but regret that our supply of campaign buttons has long been depleted and as a result I am unable to comply with your second request. Best of luck to you with your collection.

Sincerely,

Carl B. Stokes

1ˢᵗ African American Mayor of Cleveland, Ohio

My style will be management by being on the street, management by walking around. Third persons won't have to tell me what's going on in our city. I'll hear it, I'll see it, I'll touch it myself.

~C. Stokes

When you realize that people have that sort of feeling about you, that you're going to be some sort of savior from their dilemma, it's very sobering, because it imposes a great responsibility upon you.

~ C. Stokes

BLACK HISTORY 101

MOBILE MUSEUM

I knew my own situation, my own town, and I knew I had it in my hand. Once I got it, I knew I could do things that no civil rights march ever did.

~C. Stokes

It's really about schools and education. It really is about being America's safest city. I think that race is always bubbling somewhere and sometimes it does surface, but I don't think that the majority of the voters are going to pick a mayor or a candidate based solely on race.

~C. Stokes

What has been happening the last four years in City Hall is that they have been closing recreation centers, closing libraries. We have not looked after our children in City Hall.

~C. Stokes

Despite the litany of the sorrows of the city, we must believe in the ability of man to respond to the problems of his environment.

~C. Stokes

TOM BRADLEY

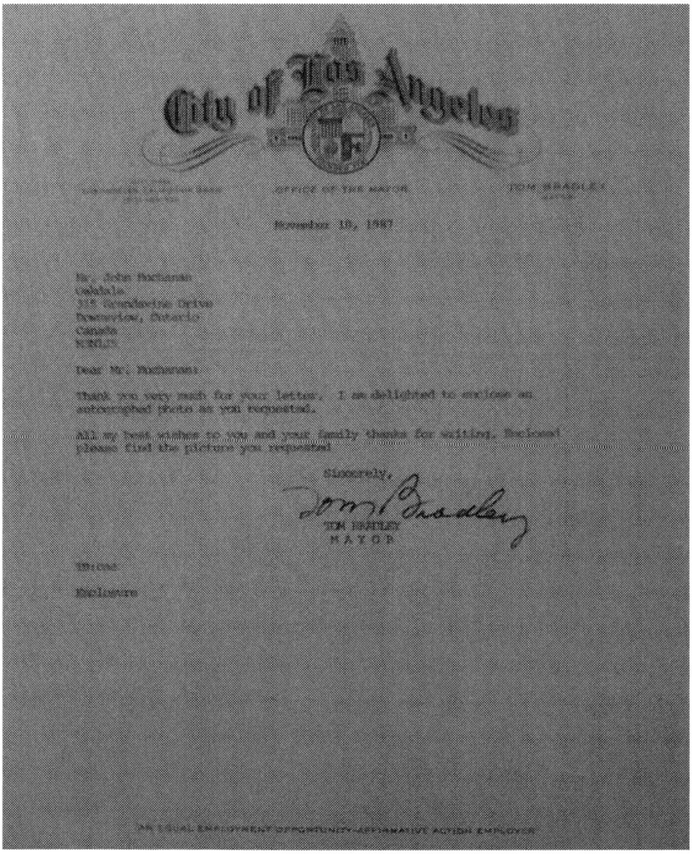

City of Los Angeles

OFFICE OF THE MAYOR

TOM BRADLEY

November 10, 1987

Mr. John [illegible]
[illegible]
[illegible] Drive
[illegible], Ontario
Canada
[illegible]

Dear Mr. [illegible]:

Thank you very much for your letter. I am delighted to enclose an autographed photo as you requested.

All my best wishes to you and your family thanks for writing. Enclosed please find the picture you requested.

Sincerely,

TOM BRADLEY
MAYOR

TB:[illegible]

Enclosure

AN EQUAL EMPLOYMENT OPPORTUNITY-AFFIRMATIVE ACTION EMPLOYER

1st African American Mayor of Los Angeles, California

The only thing that will stop you from fulfilling your dreams is you.

~T. Bradley

BLACK HISTORY 101
MOBILE MUSEUM

A loving, caring teacher took a liking to me. She noticed the potential and wanted to help shape it.

~ T. Bradley

Never give up. Keep your thoughts and your mind always on the goal.

~T. Bradley

Who bravely dares must sometimes risk a fail.

~T. Bradley

BLANCHE BRUCE

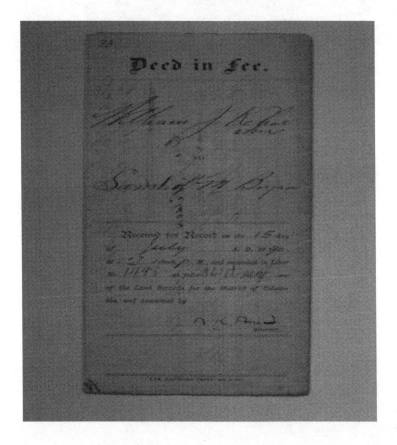

1st elected African American U.S. Senator to serve a full-term

I have confidence, not only in this country and her institutions, but in the endurance, capacity, and destiny of my people.

~B. Bruce

It will not accord with the laws of nature or history to brand colored people a race of cowards. On more than one historic field, beginning in 1776 and coming down to this centennial year of the Republic, they have attested in blood their courage as well as a love of liberty.

~B. Bruce

STxHxqjKbg

Purchase Order #: REQ-2444
Your order of May 5, 2021 (Order ID 112-1961071-4880219)

Qty.	Item	Item Price	Total
1	**Ready Player Two: A Novel** Cline, Ernest --- Hardcover **1524761338** 1524761338 9781524761332	$11.54	$11.54
1	**The Price You Pay for College: An Entirely New Road Map for the Biggest Financial Decision Your Family Will Ever Make** Lieber, Ron --- Hardcover **006286730X** 006286730X 9780062867308	$15.20	$15.20
1	**Resistance: A Songwriter's Story of Hope, Change, and Courage** Amos, Tori --- Hardcover **1982104155** 1982104155 9781982104153	$12.99	$12.99
1	**Shuggie Bain: A Novel** Stuart, Douglas --- Hardcover **0802148042** 0802148042 9780802148049	$19.29	$19.29

We've sent this part of your order to ensure quicker service. The other items will ship separately.	Subtotal	$59.02
	Promotional Certificate	-$1.92
	Shipment Total	$57.10
	Paid via credit/debit	$124.65

BARBARA JORDAN

1ˢᵗ African American woman to be elected to the U.S. House of Representatives

A nation is formed by the willingness of each of us to share in the responsibility for upholding the common good.

~B. Jordan

BLACK HISTORY 101

MOBILE MUSEUM

Education remains the key to both economic and political empowerment.

~B. Jordan

If we promise as public officials, we must deliver. If we as public officials propose, we must produce.

~B. Jordan

BLACK HISTORY 101
MOBILE MUSEUM

If you're going to play the game properly, you'd better know every rule.

~B. Jordan

SHIRLEY CHISHOLM

*1ˢᵗ African-American woman
elected to Congress*

I want history to remember me not just as the first black woman to be elected to Congress, not as the first black woman to have made a bid for the presidency of the United States, but as a black woman who lived in the 20th century and dared to be herself.

~S. Chisholm

My greatest political asset, which professional politicians fear, is my mouth, out of which come all kinds of things one shouldn't always discuss for reasons of political expediency.

~S. Chisholm

I am, was, and always will be a
catalyst for change.

~S. Chisholm

When morality comes up against profit, it is seldom profit that loses.

~S. Chisholm

EDWARD BROOKE

1ˢᵗ elected African American U.S. Senator since Reconstruction

Can education be complete without exposure to music and the arts? I believe the answer is "no". Education must include reference to men in their creative capacity, and much of the creative energy of mankind has been devoted to music and the other arts.

~E. Brooke

RALPH BUNCHE

1ˢᵗ African American to receive the Nobel Peace Prize for his mediation in the 1940's Palestine/Israeli crisis

Hearts are the strongest when they beat in response to noble ideals.

~R. Bunche

BLACK HISTORY 101

MOBILE MUSEUM

To make our way, we must have firm resolve, persistence, and tenacity. We must gear ourselves to work hard all the way. We can never let up.

~R. Bunche

We can never have too much preparation and training. We must be a strong competitor. We must adhere staunchly to the basic principle that anything less than full equality is not enough. If we compromise on that principle, our soul is dead.

~R. Bunche

We must fight as a race for everything that makes for a better country and a better world. We are dreaming idiots and trusting fools to do anything less.

~R. Bunche

COLIN POWELL

1st African American Secretary of State and 1st African American to serve on the Joint Chiefs of Staff

Many interviewers when they come to talk to me think they're being progressive by not mentioning in their stories any longer that I'm black. I tell them, 'Don't stop now. If I shot somebody you'd mention it.'

~C. Powell

There are no secrets to success. It is the result of preparation, hard work, and learning from failure.

~C. Powell

BLACK HISTORY 101
MOBILE MUSEUM

Don't be afraid to challenge the pros, even in their own backyard.

~C. Powell

Success is the result of perfection, hard work, learning from failure, loyalty, and persistence.

~C. Powell

BLACK HISTORY 101
MOBILE MUSEUM

*If you are going to achieve
excellence in big things, you develop
the habit in little matters. Excellence
is not an exception; it is a
prevailing attitude.*

~C. Powell

REV. HOSEA WILLIAMS

Civil Rights activist, Atlanta City Councilman, DeKalb County Commissioner and Georgia General Assembly legislator

~ 47 ~

We must take the power of fundamental political decision-making out of the hands of the elected officials and place it back into the hands of its rightful custodians-the people! Otherwise, selfish special-interest groups will erode the democratic process of this great republic.

~Rev. H. Williams

Development of economic and political power only brings about false security and more devastating powerlessness unless it is under-gridded with the most significant and important power--the power of self-respect.

Rev. H. Williams

It is human to be afraid, but it is inhuman to allow fear to control you.

~Rev. H. Williams

It is almost impossible to plan an acceptable future if you do not understand your unacceptable past.

~Rev. H. Williams

BLACK HISTORY 101
MOBILE MUSEUM

JOHN CONYERS

Senior African American Congressman
and one of the founders of the
Congressional Black Caucus

In this most powerful nation in the world, lack of access to health care should not force local and state governments, companies and workers into bankruptcy, while causing unnecessary illness and hospitalization.

~J. Conyers

Some of the ideas that come from the fringe of the far right are just so implausible that it is hard to take those ideas seriously.

~ J. Conyers

The American taxpayers should not have to spend one more penny on the Administration's Iraq misadventure. Let's give our troops the supplies they need to get out of Iraq safely. Let's bring our troops home.

~J. Conyers

Too many of my constituents, like many other hard working Americans across the country, are suffering unnecessarily due to our flawed health care system.

~J. Conyers

CHARLES RANGEL

*1st African American Congressman to Chair
the House Ways and Means Committee and
one of the founders of the Congressional
Black Caucus*

~ 57 ~

Full participation in government and society has been a basic right of the country symbolizing the full citizenship and equal protection of all.

~C. Rangel

I am struck by how casually we as a nation react to the carnage in Iraq.

~C. Rangel

BLACK HISTORY 101
MOBILE MUSEUM

The challenges African-Americans are facing today are rooted in the system of slavery.

~C. Rangel

There were no weapons of mass destruction and Saddam Hussein was not involved in the September 11th attack.

~C. Rangel

BLACK HISTORY 101
MOBILE MUSEUM

We love the ability of the people to influence the actions of decision-makers, of lawmakers and presidents to be removed from or elevated to office by the will of voters, and of the community to connect amongst diverse populations through the ballot box.

~C. Rangel

MAYNARD JACKSON

1ˢᵗ African American Mayor of Atlanta, Georgia

If you don't like affirmative action, what is your plan to guarantee a level playing field of opportunity?

~M. Jackson

I ran because I became convinced after King was shot and killed, and Martin Luther King was one of the great heroes of my life, that politics is not perfect but it's the best available nonviolent means of changing how we live. If we don't like how we live, we can participate in the perfect most revolutionary act in a democracy, it's called voting.

~M. Jackson

What my father and my grandfather...instilled in me is that life is an absolute waste if you're not out there on a mission that means something to humankind, the betterment of humankind. If you're only involved in making money, I was taught, if that's all your life is about, it's waste.

~M. Jackson

PATRICIA R. HARRIS

*1ˢᵗ African American woman
U.S. Ambassador*

~ 67 ~

I am a black woman, the daughter of a dining-car worker. If my life has any meaning at all, it is that those who start out as outcasts can wind up as being part of the system.

~P. Harris

JESSE JACKSON

Two-time Presidential candidate.
Founder of Rainbow/PUSH

A man must be willing to die for justice. Death is an inescapable reality and men die daily, but good deeds live forever.

~J. Jackson

*America is not a blanket woven
from one thread, one color, one cloth.*

~J. Jackson

Both tears and sweat are salty, but they render a different result. Tears will get you sympathy; sweat will get you change.

~J. Jackson

I am not a perfect servant. I am a public servant doing my best against the odds. As I develop and serve, be patient. God is not finished with me yet.

~J. Jackson

Leadership cannot just go along to get along. Leadership must meet the moral challenge of the day.

~J. Jackson

BARACK OBAMA

*1ˢᵗ African American President of
the United States of America*

I consider it part of my responsibility as President of the United States to fight against negative stereotypes of Islam wherever they appear.

~B. Obama

If you're walking down the right path and you're willing to keep walking, eventually you'll make progress.

~B. Obama

BLACK HISTORY 101

MOBILE MUSEUM

The thing about hip-hop today is it's smart, it's insightful. The way they can communicate a complex message in a very short space is remarkable.

~B. Obama

Money is not the only answer, but it makes a difference.

~B. Obama

I know my country has not perfected itself. At times, we've struggled to keep the promise of liberty and equality for all of our people. We've made our share of mistakes, and there are times when our actions around the world have not lived up to our best intentions.

~B. Obama

THURGOOD MARSHALL

*1ˢᵗ African American Supreme
Court Justice*

Ending racial discrimination in jury selection can be accomplished only by eliminating peremptory challenges entirely.

~T. Marshall

If the First Amendment means anything, it means that a state has no business telling a man, sitting alone in his house, what books he may read or what films he may watch.

~T. Marshall

In recognizing the humanity of our fellow beings, we pay ourselves the highest tribute.

~T. Marshall

BLACK HISTORY 101

MOBILE MUSEUM

None of us got where we are solely by pulling ourselves up by our bootstraps.

~T. Marshall

BLACK HISTORY 101

MOBILE MUSEUM

ADAM CLAYTON POWELL

1st African American Congressman from New York

A man's respect for law and order exits in precise relationship to the size of his paycheck.

~A. Powell

BLACK HISTORY 101
MOBILE MUSEUM

Unless man is committed to the belief that all mankind are his brothers, then he labors in vain and hypocritically in the vineyards of equality.

~A. Powell

Freedom is an internal achievement rather than an external adjustment.

~A. Powell

BLACK HISTORY 101
MOBILE MUSEUM

CAROL MOSELEY BRAUN

1st African American woman to be elected a U.S. Senator

I believe that our message of rebuilding America is one that will resonate with the American people.

~*C. Braun*

BLACK HISTORY 101
MOBILE MUSEUM

I really think that's the key, part of the spiritual renewal that America needs to have, the notion that we really can have confidence in a better tomorrow.

~C. Braun

If we can rebuild Iraq, we can rebuild Illinois and Indiana and if we can do Baghdad, we can do Baltimore.

~C. Braun

BLACK HISTORY 101
MOBILE MUSEUM

The really important victory of the civil rights movement was that it made racism unpopular, whereas a generation ago at the turn of the last century, you had to embrace racism to get elected to anything.

~*C. Braun*

MAXINE WATERS

*Congresswoman and former Chair
of the Congressional Black Caucus*

*I have a right to my anger, and I
don't want anybody telling me I
shouldn't be, that it's not nice to be,
and that something's wrong with me
because I get angry. This nation
has always struggled with how it
was going to deal
with poor people and people of
color. Every few years you will see
some great change in the way that
they approach this. We've had the
war on poverty that never really got
into waging a real war on poverty.*

~M. Waters

I've been in this struggle for many years now. I understand racism. I understand that there are a lot of people in this country who don't care about the problems of the inner city.

~ M. Waters

BLACK HISTORY 101
MOBILE MUSEUM

HAROLD WASHINGTON

1ˢᵗ African American Mayor of Chicago, Illinois

Throughout American history, many of our social gains and much of our progress toward democracy were made possible by the active intervention of the federal government.

~M. Waters

Affirmative action works but we're going to need to muster all our political resources if we are to keep it in place.

~*M. Waters*

Our concern is to heal. Our concern is to bring together.

~M. Waters

BLACK HISTORY 101

MOBILE MUSEUM

I cannot watch the city of Chicago be destroyed by petty politics and bad government.

~ M. Waters

CYNTHIA MCKINNEY

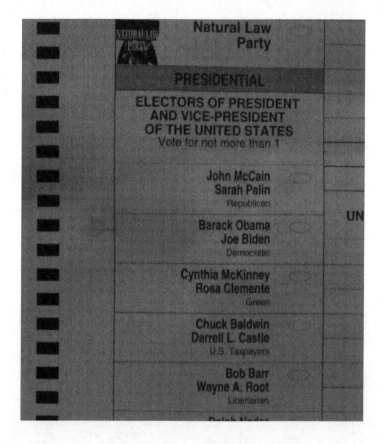

Original Presidential Ballot
1ˢᵗ African American woman to represent Georgia
in the U.S. House of Representatives. Green Party
Presidential Candidate in 2008

Eight generations of African-Americans are still waiting to achieve their rights-compensation and restitution for the hundreds of years during which they were bought and sold on the market.

~C. McKinney

In the fight against bigotry, we stand together and we must. In the fight against injustice, we stand together and we must. In the fight against intimidation, we stand together and we must. After all, a regime that would steal an election right before our very eyes will do anything to all of us.

~C. McKinney

Ever since I came to Congress in 1992, there are those who have been trying to silence my voice. I've been told to "sit down and shut up" over and over again. Well, I won't sit down and I won't shut up until the full and unvarnished truth is placed before the American people.

~C. McKinney

Images of burning Red Cross and UN buildings struck by US bombs contrasted with images of thousands of desperately poor Afghan women carrying sickly and starving children out of Afghanistan as they flee the might of the US military is tearing at international public confidence in our war against terrorism.

~C. McKinney

KEITH ELLISON

1ˢᵗ African American Muslim
elected to Congress

What we need to do as members of Congress is step up and do our job: create some jobs, put this economy in order, get some lending back to small businesses, and make this economy really work.

~ K. Ellison

Americans all across this country, they're not mad because some people are rich…they're mad because they got ripped off.

~K. Ellison

These people are outraged…We gotta be mad all together so we can restore the American dream.

~K. Ellison

BLACK HISTORY 101

MOBILE MUSEUM

Tomorrow's going to get here sooner than we think...As Americans, we need to know that as the Middle East changes, we cannot stay the same.

~K. Ellison

DAVID PATERSON

1ST African American Governor of New York

My truest disability has been my ability to overcome my physical disability.

~D. Paterson

As soon as people can see that I can be independent, then they hold me to the standard that everyone else is...

~D. Paterson

You never get to any level of leadership where your race is not a factor. You don't want to be the first; you want to be the first of many.

~D. Paterson

It's about hard work, toughness, sticking it out, picking each other up.

~D. Paterson

DAVID DINKINS

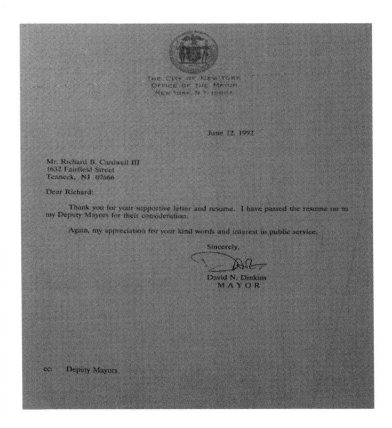

THE CITY OF NEW YORK
OFFICE OF THE MAYOR
NEW YORK, N.Y. 10007

June 12, 1992

Mr. Richard B. Cardwell III
1632 Fairfield Street
Teaneck, NJ 07666

Dear Richard:

Thank you for your supportive letter and resume. I have passed the resume on to my Deputy Mayors for their consideration.

Again, my appreciation for your kind words and interest in public service.

Sincerely,

David N. Dinkins
MAYOR

cc: Deputy Mayors

1ˢᵗ African American Mayor of New York

Ellis Island is for the people who came over here on ships. My people came over here in chains.

~D. Dinkins

BLACK HISTORY 101

MOBILE MUSEUM

Race relations can be an appropriate issue...but only if you want to craft solutions, and not catalogue complaints. If we use the issue appropriately, we can transform it from the cancer of our society into the cure.

~D. Dinkins

For too long, President Bush and the Republican Party have ignored the problems of urban America and turned their backs on the needs of our communities.

~D. Dinkins

Well, I'm not sure, but one thing I am certain: History judges one differently than contemporary observers, and so I think that as time passes, I hope that not me personally so much, but our administration will be seen for some of the things that we accomplished.

~D. Dinkins

L. DOUGLAS WILDER

1st African American to be elected Governor

I never succumb to flattery because then criticism would crush me.

~L. Wilder

The fear of error is the death of success.

~L.Wilder

BLACK HISTORY 101

MOBILE MUSEUM

ANDREW YOUNG

*1ˢᵀ African American Ambassador
to the United Nations*

~ 126 ~

You can make more money from a growing economy, than you can steal from a dying economy.

~A. Young

It is a blessing to die for a cause, because you can so easily die for nothing.

~A. Young

In a world where change is inevitable and continuous, the need to achieve that change without violence is essential for survival.

~A. Young

BLACK HISTORY 101

MOBILE MUSEUM

I have about concluded that wealth is a state of mind, and that anyone can acquire a wealthy state of mind by thinking rich thoughts.

~A. Young

Civil rights leaders are involved in helping poor people. That's what I've been doing all my life.

~A. Young

BLACK HISTORY 101
MOBILE MUSEUM

AFRICAN AMERICAN POLITICAL FIRSTS

Officeholder in colonial America: Matthias de Souza, 1641

First elected official: Wentworth Cheswell, 1776.

State elected official: Alexander Lucius Twilight, 1836.

Municipal elected official: John Mercer Langston, 1855.

U.S. ambassador: Ebenezer D. Basset, 1869.

State Supreme Court Justice: Jonathan Jasper Wright, 1870.

City mayor: Robert Wood, 1870.

U.S. Representative: Joseph Rainey, 1870.

U.S. Senator (appointed): Hiram Revels, 1870.

Governor (appointed): P.B.S. Pinchback, 1872.

Person to run for the presidency: George Edwin Taylor, 1904.

Woman legislator: Crystal Bird Fauset, 1938.

Woman U.S. Ambassador: Patricia Harris, 1965.

U.S. Senator (elected) Edward Brooke, 1966.

U.S. cabinet member: Robert C. Weaver, 1966.

Mayor of a major city: Carl Stokes (Cleveland) 1967.

Woman U.S. Representative: Shirley Chisholm, 1969.

Woman cabinet member: Patricia Harris, 1977.

U.S. Representative to the U.N.: Andrew Young, 1977.

Governor (elected): L. Douglas Wilder, 1989.

Woman mayor of a major U.S. city: Sharon Pratt Dixon Kelly, 1991.

Woman U.S. Senator, Carol Moseley Braun, 1992.

U.S. Secretary of State: Colin Powell, 2001.

Woman Secretary of State: Condoleezza Rice, 2005.

Major party nominee for President: Sen. Barack Obama, 2008.

U.S. President: Barack Obama, 2009.